TAXATION

INTERPRETING THE CONSTITUTION

— JEFF MAPUA —

New York

Published in 2015 by The Rosen Publishing Group, Inc.
29 East 21st Street, New York, NY 10010

Copyright © 2015 by The Rosen Publishing Group, Inc.

First Edition

Library of Congress Cataloging-in-Publication Data
Mapua, Jeff– author.
Taxation: interpreting the constitution/Jeff Mapua.—First edition.
pages cm.—(Understanding the United States Constitution)
Includes bibliographical references and index.
ISBN 978-1-4777-7504-2 (library bound)
1. Taxation—Law and legislation—United States—History—Juvenile literature. 2. Taxation—United States—History—Juvenile literature. I. Title.
KF6289.85.M37 2015
343.7304—dc23

                                 2013042194

Manufactured in China

CONTENTS

INTRODUCTION

PUTTING AMERICA
TO WORK

PROJECT FUNDED BY THE
American Recovery
& Reinvestment Act

The American Recovery and Reinvestment Act of 2009, a major economic stimulus package meant to lift the economy out of a severe recession, used tax dollars to fund aid to low-income workers, renewable energy research, and infrastructure projects like the one shown here.

They are argued, debated, and fought over. Lives are dedicated to defending or attacking them. They can define political theories or be used to define a social class. And, besides death, people call them the only guarantee in life.

They are taxes, and their history is full of conflict. The American Revolution itself can trace its beginnings to the colonists' reaction to a new tea tax imposed by their British rulers. Consider Al Capone. In the 1930s, the notorious gangster and mob boss was convicted not for murder or other violent crimes but for tax evasion. April 15, the day taxes are due every year in America, has become a date that many people grimly circle on their calendars and dread the approach of.

In April 2013, in the case *U.S. v. Curran*, Mary Estelle Curran faced up to six years in prison for unpaid taxes. Curran had inherited about $43 million in foreign accounts held by her husband. She pled guilty to filing false tax returns in 2006 and 2007 that did not report this inherited wealth. She was sentenced to repay nearly $22 million in penalties and almost $700,000 in overdue taxes and interest. But instead of receiving six years in prison, Curran was sentenced to five seconds of probation. The defense attorney called the sentencing unprecedented.

The complicated world of taxes can help shed light on the bizarre sentencing of Curran in what was then the biggest individual case of offshore tax evasion. The Internal Revenue Service (IRS) requires U.S. citizens to report certain financial accounts or other offshore assets. This means that when Curran inherited the accounts from her husband, she had to tell the IRS about it.

The process of telling the IRS is itself complex. There are certain requirements that need to be met. For example, the IRS Web site says, "If the total value [of the foreign assets] is at or below $50,000 at the end of the tax year, there is no reporting requirement for the year, unless the total value was more than $75,000 at any time during the tax year." Citizens who meet the requirements are required to fill out a document called Form 8938. Then there is another form that needs to be filled out, called the Report of Foreign Bank and Financial Accounts (FBAR). The FBAR form comes with its own set of requirements.

Curran's defense lawyers claimed that their client was not a savvy businesswoman who would know the complicated ins and outs of filing high-income taxes or even what forms she had to file with the IRS. They argued that when she learned about her mistakes, she took the necessary steps to immediately correct them. Luckily for Curran, the judge agreed and allowed her to avoid any jail time. The judge even went so far as to suggest she seek a pardon from the president.

Taxes have become more complicated over time. Americans need roads and highways upon which to drive their cars. Cities need police officers to help keep their streets safe and firefighters to watch over the population. Americans depend on the postal service as a means to communicate and exchange goods, information, and official and private correspondence over long distances. These public services are all essential features of a modern society. But who pays for them? Where does the money come from? And how much is a fair price for an individual to pay for these public services?

CHAPTER ONE

ON THE ROAD TO REVOLUTION: THE HOSTILE HISTORY OF TAXATION

n 1750, the American colonies were growing both in size and in wealth. Although they were still under British rule, a Swedish botanist named Peter Kalm noted that those in the colonies were said "to grow less tender" toward their ruling nation. Kalm predicted that the colonies, should they maintain their growth, would soon be able to stand on their own as an independent state.

Up until the 1760s, the colonists were still dependent on the English military for protection from French and Spanish attacks. However, after the conclusion of the French and Indian War, which raged from 1754 to 1763, France lost control of Canada and the Spanish lost control of Florida. Now with a sharply reduced need for English military protection, the American colonists would soon feel the stirrings of an independent spirit.

The thirteen colonies enjoyed a number of benefits under the British Empire. The aforementioned wealth provided many colonists with jobs. There were local governments to attend to their immediate needs. They were granted the same rights as Englishmen, such as trial by jury and other freedoms. Finally, there was no war to fight, yet there were British troops present and available for their protection. So what was it that sparked the colonists to rebel?

THE SUGAR ACT

Years of war had created a large debt for the British Empire. The national debt nearly doubled from £75,000,000 to £140,000,000. The tax system was designed in such a way that most of the debt burden was shouldered by Englishmen. American colonists were spared the expense even though they were beneficiaries of the same services as the English. The British wanted to maintain a force of one hundred thousand men to protect the American frontier. The cost of the army would be £300,000 a year. The decision was made that the colonists would have to pay for the service, since it was their own defense that was being secured.

The first attempt by the British government to raise revenue for the army was largely ignored by the

Events such as the Boston Massacre, when five colonists were killed, raised tensions between American subjects and their British rulers.

colonists, since it affected only a small portion of the population. In 1764, Parliament passed the Sugar Act. Its intention was, "Defraying the expenses of defending . . . the said colonies and plantations . . . and more effectively preventing the clandestine conveyance of goods to and from the said colonies and plantations."

George Grenville, the king's chief minister, designed the tax. The hope was to raise approximately £45,000 to help pay for the stand-ing army. At the time of the tax, the colonies had no army of their own. They depended on their local militias for defense, even though militias were poorly trained and equipped at the time.

Despite this, the colonists disagreed with the notion that the British needed a standing army based in the American colonies. Their reasoning was that there had never been a standing army before, and the colonies could defend themselves as they always had. Considering the recent removal of the French threat from the north, the colonists felt that an army was less needed than ever before. So why pay for an army that they neither needed nor wanted?

For most of the colonists, the sugar tax was not a hardship. It was primarily aimed at the merchants in the North, who were afraid that the Sugar Act would weaken several industries such as rum distillation (a process dependent upon sugar) and lumber (the export of which was restricted under the Stamp Act). While the affected merchants protested, most ordinary colonists stayed silent.

Those merchants most affected by the Sugar Act were also against the enforcement of the tax. Where smuggling had once been commonly ignored by colonial authorities, and earlier taxes like the Molasses Act of 1733 were weakly administered, the Sugar Act ushered in an era of far more aggressive efforts by colonial administrators against tax evasion.

Colonists began to wake up to the implications of the Stamp Act and protested its passage without colonial input—the taxation without representation in the British Parliament that would become such a sore spot and flashpoint in the coming years. Samuel Adams said in Boston, "If taxes are laid upon us in any shape without our having a legal Representation where they are laid, are we not reduced from the character of free Subjects to the miserable State of tributary Slaves?" This claim in particular would soon become a rallying cry.

THE STAMP ACT

The Sugar Act did not raise the amount of funds that the British rulers anticipated, and there was little relief for the taxpayers in Britain who were still paying down a large national debt. There were riots in England over the heavy tax burden, and the crown again looked to the colonies for more revenue.

In January 1765, King George III stated his intent to immediately establish the power of Great Britain to tax the colonies, no matter the opposition. The plan was to use every means in his power to enforce obedience in the colonies. In 1764, Grenville announced that the American colonists had a choice: either pay stamp duties or devise an alternative way of raising revenue. The use of a stamp tax was already in place around the world in numerous countries. However, when then Prime Minister William Pitt was asked about introducing a stamp tax to the colonies, he stated his intention never to "burn [his] fingers" on an American Stamp Act.

What is a stamp tax, exactly? It required that a stamp be attached to written and printed documents—legal documents, newspapers, printed sermons, playing cards, and much more. The British rulers expected to raise £60,000, a sum that would pay for the costs associated with maintaining an army in the American colonies. Stamps were paid for by ordinary, everyday colonists, making it the first direct tax used in the colonies. Under the Stamp Act, tax

An Emblem of the Effects of the STAMP

O! the fatal Stamp

The unpopular wax seals required by the Stamp Act were portrayed as a skull-and-crossbones in a Philadelphia newspaper.

violators would not receive a jury trial (with a jury drawn from the local population of most likely sympathetic peers) but would be tried, convicted, and sentenced by judges.

STAMPING OUT
THE STAMP ACT

In March 1765, the Stamp Act was passed by Parliament. The British government intended for the tax to take effect eight months later, but colonists condemned it long before that. Immediately after learning of the Stamp Act proposal, Americans of all classes organized and acted out in sometimes violent ways.

The Daughters of Liberty, a group consisting of women in cities, punished businesses that did not reject the act. Farmers, seamen, unskilled workers, and others united under the name Sons of Liberty. They were led by wealthier Americans, such as lawyers, who tried to coerce anyone involved with enforcing the Stamp Act to leave their positions. They carried placards that read "Liberty, Property, and No Stamps." They gathered in New York to form the Stamp Act Congress and collectively sent word to England that they would only accept taxes levied by local bodies before which their voices and viewpoints were represented and considered.

"NO TAXATION WITHOUT REPRESENTATION"

The colonies never had representatives in the British Parliament. Without representation in Parliament, it was not fair to be taxed, they argued. Colonists were outraged that, as they saw it, they could be taxed in any way and by any amount the British rulers deemed fit, without having any say in the matter.

Many in Great Britain disagreed with the colonists' reasoning that their interests and opinions were not being represented in Parliament. The British believed in a concept known as virtual representation. This doctrine said that members of Parliament represented not particular geographic areas but the economic interests of the entire empire. So although no members of Parliament came from or directly represented the colonies, the colonists were virtually represented via their economic interests. In addition, the British also believed that it was more than fair that colonists, as British subjects, should both enjoy the benefits of belonging to the empire and pay for them, just as those living in England did.

On February 13, 1766, Benjamin Franklin stood before the House of Commons and argued on behalf of the colonies. In a bit of deception, Franklin argued that the colonists' main opposition to the Stamp Act was not the stamp tax or lack of representation but the distinction between internal and external taxes. Specifically, Franklin said Americans were willing to pay taxes on imported goods but not willing to pay taxes on goods originating from the colonies. It was an interesting stance coming from a man who applied for a job selling the controversial stamps. It left the door open for taxes despite the lack of representation of the colonies in Parliament.

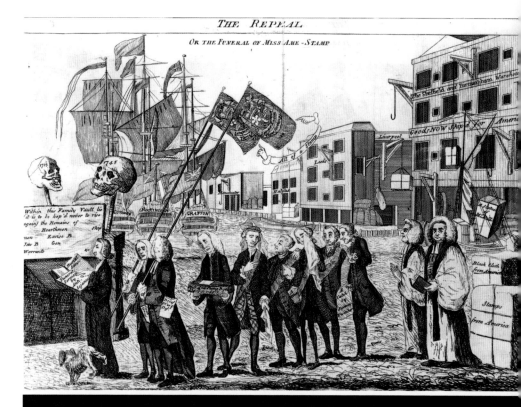

The authors of the repealed Stamp Act are shown leading their creation to its grave in this 1767 illustration.

In the end, the Stamp Act failed because of the high economic cost of the protests. Shipping firms closed, and merchants suffered losses. The new chief minister, the Marquis of Rockingham, convinced Parliament to repeal the Stamp Act. But by then the temperament in the colonies was already changing. In an ominous trend, colonists began to devote more time, care, and money on the arming and training of local militias.

TOWNSHEND REVENUE ACT

Despite the recent Stamp Act debacle, Parliament soon introduced new taxes on the colonies. Benjamin Franklin's earlier distinction between internal and external taxes came into play as Parliament took his advice and taxed goods imported from England into the colonies. The Townshend Acts of 1767 required duties charged on dyes, paper, glass, silk, and tea. They were expected to raise £40,000 to pay for English soldiers in America and other administrative costs. Parliament was happy to point out that these new taxes were acceptable under Franklin's own terms. They were perfectly consistent with Franklin's arguments while he was soliciting the repeal of the Stamp Act, one member of the cabinet pointed out.

As with the earlier Sugar and Stamp Acts, however, the colonists would challenge the new taxes. Franklin's distinction between internal and external taxes was soon dropped, and the colonists now claimed that any tax imposed by England upon the colonies required the colonies' consent. The Townshend Acts also included a requirement for Americans to house British troops and supply them with food. It further required

In response to increased costs in defending the American front of the British Empire, Parliament passed the Quartering Act. It required colonists to provide food, shelter, and transportation to British forces. This family is being forced to house and feed British soldiers against their will.

the establishment of a Board of Commissioners of Customs, which would enforce tax collection.

The combination of new taxes, housing requirements and expenses, and increased tax enforcement was too much for the colonists to accept. In fact, the revolutionary spirit that led to the ragtag colonists' unlikely rebellion against the mightiest empire in history could arguably be attributed to the oppressive enforcement of taxes as much as the taxes themselves.

Just like the Stamp Act, the Townshend Acts were repealed due to economic reasons. The Daughters of Liberty spearheaded a ban on imported English goods that led to economic suffering for many English companies and merchants. However, not all the duties associated with the Townshend Acts were lifted. The tax on tea was retained as a powerful symbol of Parliament's supremacy and its right to govern the colonies as it saw fit.

THE TEA ACT OF 1773 AND THE BOSTON TEA PARTY

After years of relative calm in the colonies following the repeal of the Sugar, Stamp, and Townshend Acts, the colonies' agitation quieted, and relative calm returned. This somewhat tense peace was again shattered, however, by the seemingly mundane issue of the price of tea in the colonies.

The British government, in an attempt to financially aid the British East India Company, exempted its tea from the remaining Townshend tea tax. This made the company's tea available at a lower price than that of Dutch tea that retained the tea tax. At this time, many American merchants sold the Dutch tea, which was commonly smuggled into the country. The British plan was to destroy the trade for Dutch tea by offering British tea at a substantially lower cost.

The Tea Act of 1773 created an issue that the colonists could rally behind. Economically, the act threatened a number of American merchants. Constitutionally, the Tea Act created a monopoly that was backed by the British government and destroyed fair competition. Taken further, the British government could then pick and choose which American companies succeeded and which failed, no doubt rewarding Loyalists and punishing anti-British merchants.

The colonists' reaction was swift and its effects long-lasting. A group of about sixty men, dressed as Mohawk Indians, boarded three tea ships in Boston. They then dumped roughly £10,000 worth of tea into Boston Harbor in protest of the Tea Act. While today the Boston Tea Party is celebrated as a turning point in America's history, at the time many colonists were shocked and condemned the actions of those sixty

About sixty men dumped chests of tea into the harbor as part of the Boston Tea Party. Although history has exaggerated the number of participants (as in the illustration shown here), it was nevertheless a key event leading to the American Revolution.

men. Benjamin Franklin wanted owners repaid for their lost tea, while many British supporters of the colonists' cause began to feel alienated from their enraged and unruly American cousins.

Eventually, the seething frustration of the colonists would lead to the American Revolution. The colonists would win out and move forward to create their own nation. Certainly, in a nation born out of a rejection of taxation, the question of taxes would always be one fraught with controversy. King

George learned from the mistakes made with the American colonies regarding taxation. He put a law in place that forbade any tax imposed on any colony to raise revenue. For the young, now independent American nation, however, a new struggle was just beginning.

CHAPTER TWO

A MORE PERFECT UNION RIVEN BY TAX REBELLION

T he revolution was won, and the former colonies had emerged as the United States of America. So now what? Having just won their independence, the citizens of the newly formed nation had to define the rules of their new country. Importantly, the question of taxation would have to be answered. The new nation would need to raise revenue to pay off its war debts, defend itself from foreign powers, and provide services to its citizens. But as King George III and the British Parliament just learned, Americans were not so easily taxed.

THE ARTICLES OF CONFEDERATION

Having just emerged from the American Revolution—a conflict sparked in large part by fury against a tyrannical government that sought to impose and enforce unpopular tax policy—the authors of the new nation's laws sought to limit the powers of a centralized government. In 1781, after much deliberation, the thirteen states approved the Articles of Confederation, as they came to be called. The states created their own governments, loosely presided over by a weak central government. Even at the state level, the executive branch was weak compared to the state legislatures. For example, state governors were stripped of the power to veto and make appointments and had terms of only one year. Pennsylvania actually did away with the office of governor altogether.

Wary of the government's power to tax, the newly created U.S. Congress was not granted revenue-raising power, though it could pass tax measures with a supermajority agreement. This meant that to raise revenue, Congress had to ask the states for money. To pass the measure, nine of the thirteen states had to approve the tax. Compared to the British Parliament, where a simple majority of the members was required for approval of a proposed measure, the supermajority rule made it very difficult to pass any tax, let alone abuse the tax system, exercise discrimination, or overspend.

The taxation system under the Articles of Confederation was summarized by the nation's chief

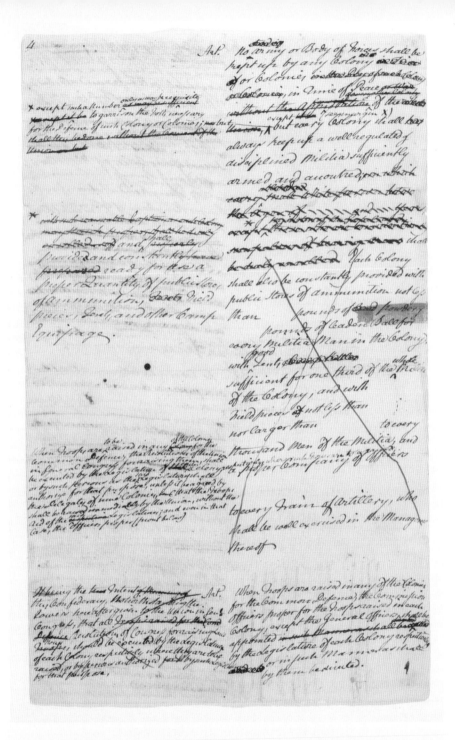

Following their experience with British tyranny, the authors of the Articles of Confederation were intent on limiting the powers of the central government of the new American nation. A handwritten draft of the Articles appears here.

financial officer, Robert Morris, when he complained that the Congress had the "privilege of asking for everything, but the states were given the prerogative of granting nothing. With no money and no way to raise it, the United States faced mounting debts and fiscal failure before the country was even out of the earliest days of its infancy.

SHAYS'S REBELLION

Unfortunately for the citizens of the United States, the economy would only get worse. Among the problems was a serious economic depression that settled in by 1784. The United States was not allowed to enjoy the benefits of trading with the English and their remaining colonies as Americans had before the revolution. As punishment for their successful rebellion, American merchants were now forced to pay heavy duties on English goods.

Many states enacted "stay" laws that prevented the collection of debts, and they put a hold on the collecting of taxes. However, Massachusetts was not one of those states. It continued to collect taxes, and it set the tax rate high in order to pay off its war debts. The taxes were too much to bear for some people. The only choice they felt they had was rebellion, and one broke out in 1786.

In response to the aggressive tax enforcement and regulations imposed by what Massachusetts citizens considered a tyrannical state government, Daniel Shays led thousands of people in revolt. History shows that struggling farmers and even those wealthy enough to afford the taxes joined together to protest the economic hardship placed upon them. Shays, a former captain of the Continental Army, prevented the courts from foreclosing on farms due to nonpayment of taxes. Only after Shays's rebels attempted to seize a federal supply of weapons were they repelled by the Massachusetts militia and the violence put to an end.

Following Shays's Rebellion, there were calls to fix the Articles of Confederation. Congress needed the power to tax the states and citizenry despite the fact

This wood engraving depicts Massachusetts militiamen firing on a group of men participating in Shays's Rebellion in Springfield, Massachusetts, in 1786.

that the majority of Americans opposed the concept. One thing was for sure—the system wasn't working, and something had to change.

THE U.S. CONSTITUTION

"The Congress shall have Power To lay and collect Taxes, Duties, Imposts and Excises, to pay the Debts and provide for the common Defence and General Welfare of the United States; but all Duties, Imposts and Excises shall be uniform throughout the United States." —Article 1, Section 8, Clause 1 of the Constitution of the United States

In May 1787, representatives from twelve states, minus Rhode Island, convened in Philadelphia to solve the riddle of how strong the central government should be and whether or not it should be granted the power to tax. Fifty-five delegates attended the Constitutional Convention. George Washington pre-sided over the debates. Rather than making changes to the existing Articles of Confederation, those at the convention agreed to create an entirely new constitution.

In addition to creating a stronger central govern-ment and executive branch led by a president, the delegates agreed to retain the powers Congress had received under the Articles of Confederation. The very first power granted the new Congress was the power to tax. In a concession to the southern states and their concern over the tobacco trade, Congress would not be able to levy taxes on exports, but it had the power to regulate commerce. Importantly, taxes had to be uniform throughout the United States. In France, the citizens would soon engage in their own revolution,

The Constitution replaced the Articles of Confederation as the fundamental law of the land and a document that both defines the structure of federal government, its powers, its responsibilities, and its limits.

and one of the root causes was tax discrimination that favored one class of citizen over another. Wisely, the delegates of the Constitutional Convention avoided any such pitfalls in the tax law. The authors of the Constitution were careful to include phrases such as "uniform and equal" to make their intentions regarding fair taxation clear.

Many saw direct taxation as dangerous. They feared it could lead to citizens paying more than their fair share. The founders' solution was a concept called apportionment. Taxes were calculated according to the population of a region. Supporters of apportionment claimed it avoided citizens paying more than their proportionate share.

Direct taxes (taxes paid directly to the government by the persons on whom it is imposed) would be used only in the most extreme situations, or as James Madison said, in an extraordinary emergency. The distrust of direct taxation was not new in the history of governments. The ancient Greeks and Romans equated direct taxes with tyranny and believed it should only be used to avoid total economic and social collapse. After about a century, however, the United States would soon come to rely upon and accept direct taxation as a normal way of life.

Another feature of the Constitution that has changed over the years was the requirement that taxes could only be used to pay for debts, defense, and "the general Welfare." Alexander Hamilton explained this feature as "tying up the hands of government from offensive wars founded upon reasons of state." Wars, he reasoned, cost too much. "The general Welfare" referred to not using tax money for local benefits or special interests.

THE CONSTITUTION: CONSENTED TO BUT NOT EMBRACED

The Constitution was not universally accepted by all the delegates and was not passed without reservation. Anti-Federalists believed the federal government would gain too much power at the expense of the states under the new Constitution. They feared that the executive branch would come to wield power similar to a king. Benjamin Franklin stated that he doubted the Constitution would endure and that it might lead to tyranny in the executive branch. He lent his support to the document nevertheless because he felt it was the best available option and he didn't expect a better one to come along.

SIN TAXES AND THE WHISKEY REBELLION OF 1791

In May 1790, Rhode Island was the last state to ratify the Constitution. It would not be long before there were challenges to lawmakers creating taxes in its name. As the new secretary of the treasury, Alexander Hamilton convinced Congress to institute a tax on whiskey to help pay off debts from the war. In his view, the tax was a "sin tax," since whiskey was a luxury and taxing alcohol would help curb the nation's unhealthy drinking habits. The Revenue Act of 1789 set a tariff on imports at 8 percent, a number too low in Hamilton's opinion. The whiskey tax, among taxes on other goods, would help add to revenue.

The Whiskey Rebellion was one of the earliest revolts against taxation in the United States. Rebels sometimes tarred and feathered tax collectors as part of their protests.

This excise tax (a tax on a good or product) was instantly unpopular. Just as in colonial days, government workers who attempted to collect on the whiskey tax were tarred and feathered by angry citizens. Farmers in the backcountry of Pennsylvania saw the tax as an unfair burden placed on them specifically. Many used whiskey for bartering, so the whiskey tax was for them a tax on their forms of currency and trade. What was a luxury for others was a necessity—a form of money—to the farmers. Additionally, they claimed that the tax was not uniform because the cotton and tobacco of southern planters were not being similarly taxed.

The Whiskey Rebellion included acts of violence against tax collectors. In one instance, protestors were killed and soldiers injured in a skirmish in western Pennsylvania. This may have been a step too far for the rebels, and many backed off their protests. However, President George Washington, at the request of Hamilton, rode out to meet the remaining rebels in full military attire. Washington wanted to show Americans and those watching from afar that his new country and its government, though young, would not be trifled with.

More for show than in the interests of actual justice, several rebels were arrested and sentenced to be hanged. Later, Washington pardoned all involved. Although the rebels were defeated, the whiskey tax was eventually repealed soon after Thomas Jefferson was elected president.

TAX CHALLENGE: *HYLTON V. UNITED STATES*

A new challenge to the Constitution came not on the battlefield but in a courtroom. One of the earliest challenges to the new taxation powers of Congress arose from a carriage tax on passenger vehicles. In Virginia, Daniel Hylton refused to pay the carriage tax on the grounds that it was a direct tax. Article I, Section 8 of the Constitution required the government to apportion taxes based on population, and Hylton's defense claimed that the tax violated this requirement. The constitutionality of the tax was therefore called into question.

The lower courts were divided in their opinions. The decision became the burden of three justices of the Supreme Court: Samuel Chase, James Iredell, and William Paterson. In the end, it was unanimously decided that the carriage surcharge was an indirect tax and within the government's taxation rights laid out in the Constitution. The new government's law held up in court against this early challenge.

This case was the first in U.S. history in which the Supreme Court assumed power to nullify unconstitutional acts of Congress. Although the first case in which the Supreme Court explicitly stated this power and overturned an act of Congress would come later, *Hylton* was a landmark case on its own. The fact that the first of such cases in U.S. history dealt with taxation should come as no surprise. The decision of the three justices would set a precedent for over one hundred years.

CHAPTER THREE

TAXES, SECTIONALISM, AND THE CIVIL WAR

A lthough the United States had a new Constitution, and a more effective distribution of powers between the federal government and the states had been agreed upon, new challenges would arise as the new Congress's laws were put to the test.

Following the election of John Adams as president, Congress passed the first direct tax. The tax was on lands and slaves. Additionally, houses were taxed based on their number of doors and windows. As government workers counted the windows and doors of houses in eastern Pennsylvania, German settlers drove them out. These tax rebels were arrested but later freed by a sympathizer named John Fries.

Just as the Whiskey Rebellion ended with militia involvement, so, too, did Fries Rebellion. Fries was pardoned, but the damage was done. It had become clear that the tax policies of the early United States would have to conform to the will of citizens.

Using a different, nonviolent tactic, Daniel Hylton, who owned 125 carriages but refused to pay taxes on any of them, questioned the taxation powers of the federal government on constitutional grounds. As the nation matured, there would be more of these kinds of legal challenges to the Constitution. Though the guns and violence of the colonial and early post-revolutionary-era tax protests were exchanged for lawyers and court-rooms, the battle over taxes remained the same.

TAX CHALLENGE: *MCCULLOCH V. MARYLAND*

In 1791, Alexander Hamilton proposed the creation of a federal bank. The First Bank of the United States, as it was to be called, had many opponents, such as James Madison and Thomas Jefferson. The two legendary figures claimed that the bank was a direct violation of the Constitution. Eventually, the proponents of the bank won out with the condition that its charter would last for only twenty years.

The First Bank of the United States was the country's first-ever federal or national bank. Alexander Hamilton supported the creation of the bank, believing it would stabilize and improve the nation's credit and improve the government's financial management and operations. Others, like Thomas Jefferson, opposed the institution, fearing it would grant too much power and influence to the federal government.

The bank's charter was renewed in 1816, however, despite the opposition of numerous powerful members of Congress. Many states also opposed the bank. In a form of protest, the states created new taxes on the bank's branches. Maryland, in particular, adopted a statute in 1818 that imposed a tax on banks operating in the state that were "not chartered by the [state] legislature."

James McCulloch, head of the Baltimore branch of the national bank, refused to pay the state tax and challenged the state's ability to tax an instrument of the federal government. Also in question was the meaning of the Necessary and Proper Clause of the U.S. Constitution and the power of the federal government to incorporate a bank.

Regarding the power to incorporate a bank, chief justice of the Supreme Court John Marshall concluded that it was within the rights of the federal government to do so. Based on a loose interpretation of the Constitution, he argued that although the power to create a bank was not explicitly stated, it was an "incidental or implied" power. Further, the bank was a necessary instrument for the government to impose and collect taxes and regulate commerce, both duties sanctioned by the Constitution.

On the issue of a state's power to tax agencies of the federal government, Marshall was clear. He stated that federal law was supreme and the states were subordinate. The drafters of the Constitution did not intend to make their government dependent on the states, Marshall said. He reasoned that if a state were able to tax the federal bank, then states could tax the mail, federal courts, and so on. The power to tax involves the power to destroy, he declared, and the states could thereby destroy all government efforts, initiatives, and purposes should the power to tax federal agencies remain.

There were opponents of Marshall's decision. They felt it gave too much power to the national government, that the bank was not operating in the nation's best interests, and that the loose interpretation of the Constitution set a dangerous precedent. By 1828, when Andrew Jackson became president, the end of the bank's second charter was near. Jackson was a proponent of states' rights and vetoed the bill to recharter the bank. However, attitudes changed after the Civil War, and *McCulloch v. Maryland* remains an important precedent that continues to influence the debate over the federal government's role in the economy today.

SECTIONALISM AND THE TARIFFS ERA

As the Federalist Party lost power, the way the United States taxed its citizens gradually changed. Rather

LOUGHBOROUGH V. BLAKE

In a less influential but still important case, *Loughborough v. Blake* brought up the question of taxation without representation. The main issue of the case was whether the federal government had the right to collect taxes in Washington, D.C.

The District of Columbia is not a state, and, as such, does not have a representative in Congress. Yet the government wanted to tax the citizens of the

The phrase "taxation without representation" became an important rallying cry in the American Revolution and beyond. Today, it graces the license plates of Washington, D.C., drivers, reflecting the District's unique political status within the Union.

federal district. Prior to the American Revolution, taxing those without representatives in the governing body was unthinkable. Certainly, the phrase "no taxation without representation" became a major rallying cry of the rebelling American colonists. However, Chief Justice Marshall and his fellow justices unanimously agreed that it was within the powers of Congress to collect taxes within the District of Columbia.

Their reasoning was that the powers of Congress extend to all places where the government executes law. Marshall made the point that the colonies had no common interest with England, separated as they were by a vast ocean and not bound together by any common feelings, while the District of Columbia suffered no such alienation or estrangement from the United States.

than raising revenue by taxing the people, a tariff was introduced in 1816 to bolster the manufacturing of American goods and protect American industry from the importation of cheap foreign goods. The tariff, which would be applied to any foreign manufactured goods, was designed to reduce the federal deficit that had ballooned during the War of 1812.

The Tariff of 1816 was initially supported by states in both the North and the South. Northern states, where manufacturing was the main component of the economy, supported the measure because it made their products more affordable and desirable. Ordinarily, southern states would have opposed the measure because they were large consumers of foreign manufactured goods, and the tariff would make these more expensive. In this case, however, the South, worried about both the deficit and England's attempt to dominate American markets for manufactured goods, threw its support behind the tariff. The tariff was passed only by the slimmest of margins as nationalism won over local interests. However, what little support the tariff initially enjoyed was eroded by 1820.

Led by Congressman John C. Calhoun (representing South Carolina), the state of South Carolina claimed that the tariff favored northern manufacturers while punishing southern farmers. This divide between the two regions introduced sectionalism, or exaggerated devotion to one's region, in the United States.

While debating the federal government's plan to use money from the tariff to build roads and canals for transportation, protestors challenged the power of Congress to, according to the Constitution, "lay and collect taxes," "provide for the common defense and general welfare," and pass laws "necessary and proper for carrying into execution the foregoing powers." Those opposed to the tariff believed these powers

Southern politicians like South Carolina Congressman John C. Calhoun championed states' rights and sought to nullify many federal laws, including those related to what they viewed as unfair, regionally discriminatory taxation.

were too vague and too "elastic." Simply, they believed that only the explicitly stated powers granted by the Constitution were legal. Unfortunately for the protestors, the tariff was not only not abolished but was actually increased in 1824.

Cooperation between northern and southern states grew even more strained with the 1828 tariff, dubbed by its foes the "Tariff of Abomination." Once again, in an attempt to protect and bolster northern manufacturing interests, this tariff required a tax on imported goods. The import tax made southerners pay higher prices for the goods bought primarily from England. When the importation of British goods slowed as a result, England, in turn, could no longer afford to buy southern cotton. Just as with the Tariff of 1816, southerners claimed that this new tariff favored northern merchants over southern farmers.

Regional tension was higher than ever before and reached a tipping point with the passage of the Tariff of 1832. Moving forward with a threat made by Calhoun in earlier debates, South Carolina nullified, or made legally void, the Tariffs of 1828 and 1832 (Calhoun was vice president of the United States at this time, serving under John Quincy Adams and Andrew Jackson). Even though the Tariff of 1832 actually lowered the tax, South Carolina remained committed to nullification.

Only after military intervention by President Andrew Jackson did the nullification crisis come to an end. In the wake of the tariff controversy, however, taxes remained a cause of controversy and regional sectionalism, with South Carolina even threatening to secede from the Union.

RAISING MONEY FOR WAR

The first income tax in U.S. history was passed in 1861 and applied to the northern states of the Union following the secession of the southern Confederate states. It was a flat tax set at 3 percent for incomes over $800, or about $21,000 in today's dollars. The new secretary of the treasury for President Abraham Lincoln, Salmon P. Chase, suggested that the costs associated with the Civil War would approach $240 million, and the Revenue Tax of 1861 would help pay for it. Not only was his estimate too conservative, but the new income tax also did little to raise revenue. Historians estimate that only 3 percent of the population paid this tax, and collecting the money proved to be enormously challenging and problematic.

In 1862, the Bureau of Internal Revenue was created to help oversee and collect the new income tax. By the beginning of 1863, the new office had almost four thousand employees, including collectors and

To pay for the Civil War, the first national income tax was enacted. In this illustration, taxpayers stand in line to pay income taxes for the first time in U.S. history.

assessors. An updated version of the income tax was passed in 1862. It introduced a progressive tax by exempting those with incomes less than $600 from paying any taxes. Those with incomes between $600 and $10,000 would pay 3 percent, while those with incomes over $10,000 would pay 5 percent. This proved again to raise too little revenue, and in 1864 the rates were increased from 3 to 8 percent for middle-income earners, and from 5 to 10 percent for high-income earners.

In a country so opposed—often violently—to taxes, how was the government able to push through an income tax? First, the Revenue Act of 1862 was explicitly presented as a temporary measure. Second, many Northerners saw the Civil War as a fight not only for the Union, but also for the principle of democratic government by the people. Supporters argued that the tax was only a small percentage of a person's income and, ultimately, a small price to pay to fight slavery and save the Union. The North won the war, but the battle over taxes would rage on.

TAX CHALLENGE: *SPRINGER V. UNITED STATES*

Almost twenty years after the Civil War, a legal battle was fought over income tax. In 1881, the Revenue Act of 1864 was challenged in the case *Springer v. United States*. Stemming from a failure to pay his income tax beginning in 1864, William M. Springer sued the government when his properties were seized as partial repayment on his back taxes.

Springer's claim was that the income tax was prohibited by the Constitution on the grounds that it was a direct tax. Again, the question of apportionment arose. The Supreme Court ruled that only taxes on

real estate and capitation (a tax levied by the government upon a person at a fixed rate regardless of
income or worth) were direct taxes. The unanimous
7–0 ruling on January 24, 1881, stated that income
taxes were indirect taxes based on geographical uniformity and therefore permitted under the
Constitution. Although the ruling helped define
income tax, a case in 1895 would once again muddy
the issue.

TAX CHALLENGE: *POLLOCK V. FARMERS' LOAN & TRUST CO.*

Pollock v. Farmers' Loan & Trust Co. called into
question the income tax law of 1894. The law taxed
income over $4,000 at 2 percent and made securities
and corporate profits subject to this tax. It was the
first attempt to tax income in peacetime. It was a
small step toward addressing a widening wealth gap
among American citizens due to an expanding industrial economy. Opponents of the new tax law claimed
it was unconstitutional and sought court protection
against what they claimed was government-mandated
wealth redistribution.

In 1895, a stockholder sued to keep his bank from
paying the income tax. The bank's lawyers claimed
that the income levy was a direct tax forbidden by the

Constitution (which required that taxes be apportioned, not direct). By a vote of 5–4 in the Supreme Court, the tax was invalidated on the basis that it was indeed a direct tax.

While the income tax law of 1894 was struck down, the Sixteenth Amendment introduced in the next century would soon turn tax policy upside down once again.

CHAPTER FOUR

A NEW ERA AND A NEW DEAL

The era of taxation during the Civil War introduced the concept of income taxes to the United States. During that volatile time, extra money was needed to pay for soldiers, weapons, food, and all the necessities of an army, in addition to the everyday needs of running a country. The war would decide the future of slavery and the economic health and long-term prospects of the North and South. Considering the grave and urgent importance of these issues, taxing income could be seen as a necessary, if temporary, measure.

The end of the war would raise new questions about the ongoing necessity of an income tax. With the turn of the century, it would soon become the major issue of the era. America would then fall deep into an economic depression, and government spending would rise to a level never seen before.

FLINT V. STONE TRACY COMPANY

In 1909, Congress introduced a new corporate tax. The tax included all income earned by a corporation, including the proceeds of investments. In 1911, the corporate tax was challenged in the case *Flint v. Stone Tracy Company*.

The claim was that the income of a corporation fell outside the scope of the federal government, and only the states were able to tax corporate income. Additionally, the old argument of direct tax versus apportioned tax was raised once again. The Supreme Court ruled, however, that the federal income tax on corporations was legal, as was the including of state securities and investments in this taxable income. The reasoning was that the corporate tax was an indirect tax. In the wake of this ruling, income tax was now applicable to corporations as well as to individuals.

THE SIXTEENTH AMENDMENT

"The Congress shall have power to lay and collect taxes on incomes, from whatever source derived, without apportionment among the several States, and without regard to any census or enumeration."

Sixty-first Congress of the United States of America;

At the First Session,

Begun and held at the City of Washington on Monday, the fifteenth day of March,
one thousand nine hundred and nine.

JOINT RESOLUTION

Proposing an amendment to the Constitution of the United States.

*Resolved by the Senate and House of Representatives of the United States
of America in Congress assembled (two-thirds of each House concurring
therein),* That the following article is proposed as an amendment to the
Constitution of the United States, which, when ratified by the legislatures of
three-fourths of the several States, shall be valid to all intents and purposes as a
part of the Constitution:

"ARTICLE XVI. The Congress shall have power to lay and collect taxes
on incomes, from whatever source derived, without apportionment among the
several States, and without regard to any census or enumeration."

Speaker of the House of Representatives.

*Vice-President of the United States and
President of the Senate.*

Attest:

Clerk of the House of Representatives.

Charles G. Bennett

By Henry H. Gilfry,
Secretary

The controversial Sixteenth Amendment to the Constitution allowed the U.S. government to tax income. This resolution formally announces the proposal of the amendment that would be adopted in 1913.

These few lines from the Sixteenth Amendment changed the way the federal government could tax citizens. In 1909, the amendment—proposed to settle the question of the constitutionality of an income tax once and for all—passed Congress and required ratification from the states before acquiring the force of law. Supporters of the income tax pointed to a similar income tax used successfully by the British. Fears of putting American liberty at risk were calmed with the offering of evidence that a properly administered income tax could be beneficial to the nation and all its citizens.

Though opponents claimed that the income tax was merely the exercise of tyranny through legislation, the mood in America had changed, and an income tax was welcomed. The Sixteenth Amendment removed the requirement that taxes be apportioned, and the income tax was exempted from the constitutional prohibition against direct taxes.

Government revenue from traditional sources such as excise taxes, tariffs, and customs duties fell with the passage of the Sixteenth Amendment and the opening up of a new funding stream. Congress passed a new income tax once the Sixteenth Amendment was ratified and took effect. The Bureau of Internal Revenue added a Personal Income Tax division. In 1913, the tax rates were set at 1 to 6 percent on individuals

PROGRESSIVE TAX VS. FLAT TAX

There are two different ways income has been taxed in the United States. A flat tax was introduced first, and the progressive tax was adopted later. A flat tax sets an equal tax rate across all levels of income. This means that an individual who earns $100 will pay the same percentage as an individual who earns $10,000. Supporters of a flat tax celebrate the uniformity of the tax. Not only would everyone pay the same percentage, but also different types of

Some taxpayers have no love for the IRS, like this citizen protesting outside of the James C. Corman Federal Building in California.

economic activities would be taxed equally. There would be no tax penalty for earning more, thus creating an incentive to gain more wealth. Another benefit is that filing taxes would become simpler for taxpayers, and agencies could regulate the taxes more easily.

Opponents of the flat tax, however, claim that the current progressive income tax—in which higher earners pay a higher percentage of their income in taxes—raises more revenue than a flat tax system would. This means, should flat taxes be adopted today, the tax rate on higher earners would decrease and, as a result, tax rates would have to be raised on lower-income earners to make up for the shortfall.

A progressive tax sets tax rates higher for additional income. Progressive taxes are justified by the fact that the poor do not have as much income to tax, and a dollar from someone without much costs more than taking the same dollar from a person with millions of dollars. The fear is that, without a progressive tax, a small minority of citizens will possess and control the vast majority of the nation's wealth. Opponents say a progressive tax reduces incentive to gain wealth, threatens economic expansion, and is a form of socialism.

(depending on their income level). Corporate income was taxed at 1 percent.

The progressive nature of the Revenue Act of 1913 defined levels of income, each of which is taxed higher as income rises. The tax was designed in such a way that only about 5 percent of the population was affected by it. In effect, it was a tax on the wealthy.

TAX CHALLENGE: *BRUSHABER V. UNION PACIFIC RAILROAD*

Uniformity of taxes was required by Article I, Section 8 of the Constitution. In the case *Brushaber v. Union Pacific Railroad*, the U.S. Supreme Court addressed whether or not the Revenue Act of 1913 levied taxes uniformly.

The 1916 case forced the Court to explain how a tax that affected only about 5 percent of the population was considered uniformly applied. The Supreme Court made clear that Article I, Section 8 required only geographic uniformity—meaning a proportional amount of people were being taxed in every part of the country—not uniformity in the sense that every citizen was being taxed at the same rate.

As time went on, the Revenue Act of 1913 would be strengthened with increases in the tax percentages. By World War II, a majority of Americans were affected by the income tax. Fewer exemptions were made for low-income earners, and the highest tax rates rose to 50 percent. They would eventually rise to as high as 91 percent.

PAYING FOR WORLD WAR I

As World War I began, the United States needed to raise revenue for the war effort. In September 1914, President Woodrow Wilson asked Congress to raise $100 million (nearly $2 billion in today's dollars) to help finance the war. Rather than imposing a tax on imports, President Wilson asked for an internal, or domestic, tax.

By November of the same year, Congress passed the War Revenue Tax Act of 1914. The act introduced—in some cases reintroduced—various excise taxes on goods such as liquor, wine, chewing gum, and toilet articles. Bankers, brokers, amusement park owners, and those in the tobacco industry were also taxed.

A stamp tax was also passed. This version of the stamp tax required 5 cents on every $100 of certificates of stock. Like the income taxes introduced during the Civil War, these taxes were temporary, expiring about one year after they would take effect. However, when the time came for the taxes to expire, Congress extended the taxes. The extension would not last long.

In July 1916, Representative Claude Kitchin of North Carolina introduced a bill to raise another $200 million for the war effort. The Emergency

American soldiers were sent to Europe to fight in World War I. Taxes had to be raised to help pay for their transportation, uniforms, weapons, ammunition, food, and medical care.

Revenue Act of 1916, as it was called, was passed on September 8, 1916. It repealed the War Revenue Tax Act of 1914, ending the latter act's extension.

The Emergency Revenue Act increased income taxes and taxes on corporations. It even taxed illegal businesses, such as bootlegging and gambling. Many federal and state employees—including the president—were exempt. Estates and trusts were taxed for the first time. For investors, dividends were defined as money from a company's earnings paid out to stockholders, and these were taxed.

A final War Revenue Act of 1917 became law on October 3, 1917. Income was taxed at a higher rate, and even more goods and types of income, such as stocks, were taxed. The income tax hike was encouraged by government employees who convinced citizens that if they paid their taxes promptly and in full, they would help defeat the nation's enemies overseas.

THE GREAT DEPRESSION AND THE NEW DEAL

On March 4, 1933, President Franklin Delano Roosevelt was sworn into office and the worst depression in American history was waiting for him. His predecessor, Herbert Hoover, had attempted to rescue the country from the Great Depression, by among other things, raising taxes at a higher rate than ever before with the Revenue Act of 1932, but his measures were of little help. Twenty-five percent of the population was unemployed, the gross national product (GNP) was cut in half, and the banking system collapsed. Roosevelt had to find a way to get the homeless and people in bread lines back to work. No help would come from countries abroad, as they were in equally terrible shape.

During his inauguration, Roosevelt gave hope back to the people, famously declaring, "The only thing we have to fear is fear itself." His solution was the New Deal, a wide-reaching series of economic stimulus programs. He immediately addressed the broken financial system. Bankers were found to have

The Great Depression made it difficult for families to find food to eat. Many of the homeless and unemployed had no choice but to stand in long lines, waiting for hours to obtain a free loaf of bread or a bowl of soup.

committed fraud, left taxes unpaid, been granted hidden bonuses, provided unethical loans, and more. As part of Roosevelt's banking reform efforts, acts such as the Glass-Steagall Banking Act separated investment from commercial banking and instituted the federal insurance of bank deposits.

On June 16, 1933, the National Industrial Recovery Act (NIRA) became law. It was hailed by Roosevelt as "the most important and far-reaching legislation ever enacted by the American Congress." Large-scale public works projects began, putting Americans back to work and generating much-needed spending and income. Among many other changes, dividends were now taxed at 5 percent, though by December 31, 1933, Roosevelt terminated the dividend tax provision. However, other taxes were introduced, such as the Beer and Wine Revenue Bill, a gasoline tax, and a cotton ginning tax. Existing income and liquor taxes were increased. By 1933, the economy showed early signs of recovery.

In 1935, Roosevelt raised taxes on the rich. He believed that the wealthy benefitted from advantages provided by the government, and it was his duty to "restrict such incomes by very high taxes." Those with incomes of $5 million a year—$78 million in today's dollars—were taxed at 79 percent. This tax reportedly applied to only one person, John D. Rockefeller Jr.

SOCIAL SECURITY

In the case *A.L.A. Schechter Poultry Corp. v. United States*, President Roosevelt saw his National Industrial Recovery Act ruled unconstitutional. The NIRA required the live poultry industry to establish a fifty-cents-an-hour minimum wage and forty-hour work-week. The Supreme Court wanted to slow the government's regulation over commerce and strike down what it viewed as an uncon-stitutional code for the poultry industry. Roosevelt was enraged over the decision and responded with a new social welfare program called Social Security.

In 1937, the first Social Security taxes

Machines take on the enormous task of stamping checks for Social Security recipients at the Division of Disbursement in 1939, the first year that Social Security payments began to be issued.

were collected. As a payroll tax, Social Security paid for insurance for the aged and unemployed. Originally, employers and employees paid 1 percent of the first $3,000 of salaries and wages. Social Security was a significant tax increase on the employed. For three years before Social Security began making payments to retired, elderly, and unemployed Americans, the economy suffered a recession.

The creation of Social Security was a sign that the government aligned itself with laborers and workers' unions. It guaranteed a minimum level of comfort and financial security to the elderly and vulnerable that had previously been lacking. By 1999, Social Security taxes accounted for 32 percent of all federal revenue.

TAX CHALLENGE: *STEWARD MACHINE COMPANY V. DAVIS*

On May 24, 1937, the Supreme Court decided the case *Steward Machine Company v. Davis*. The Charles C. Steward Machine Company of Alabama sued Harwell G. Davis, Alabama's collector of internal revenue, over $46.14 paid for the Social Security tax. The company claimed that the Social Security Act was unconstitutional because some of its provisions went beyond the powers granted to Congress by the Constitution. It further claimed that the act violated the states' powers granted by the Tenth Amendment and forced states to adopt Social Security whether they wanted to or not.

In a narrow vote of 5–4, the Supreme Court justices validated the Social Security Act. The Court argued that the act was within Congress's power "to lay and collect taxes" and provide for general welfare. Notably, the *Steward* decision supported welfare programs run by both the federal and state governments.

CHAPTER FIVE

THE MODERN FIGHT

The New Deal had introduced a new attitude toward taxation. Banks and the wealthy became targets of taxes as the middle and lower classes gained political power. By century's end, however, the wealthy would once again be the beneficiaries of generous tax breaks, while the working and middle classes shouldered a disproportionately heavy tax burden.

PAYING FOR WORLD WAR II

In the 1940s, taxation expanded when the United States again became involved in a world war. The wealthy were already taxed at a higher rate than ever before, so there would not be much revenue gained by raising taxes on the upper class. At this time, only 3 percent of Americans paid income taxes. The obvious solution was to institute income taxes among the middle and working classes.

The World War II–era tax increases saw the bottom rate increase from 4 to 23 percent on incomes over $500 (about $6,000 in today's dollars). On the other end of the wage scale, incomes above $200,000 (about $2.4 million today) were taxed at 94 percent. The number of people paying income taxes increased during the war. By 1942, thirty-four million Americans were paying taxes on income, so the Bureau of Internal Revenue educated Americans about the tax system. Most households accepted the necessity of income tax during wartime.

Congress passed the 1942 Revenue Act, a tax increase and extension that President Roosevelt called "the greatest tax bill in American history." However, the tax system became more complex with various exemptions, provisions, and deductions. Despite his support of the tax, Roosevelt commented, "The bill might as well have been written in a foreign language."

There were other taxes created to help pay for the war. In February 1944, the Revenue Act was made into law. The excess profit tax rate and other excise taxes were increased. Roosevelt was able to simplify income tax with the Individual Income Tax Act of 1944. While it reduced taxes overall, it also expanded income tax to include nearly all Americans. In the end, the government's goal of

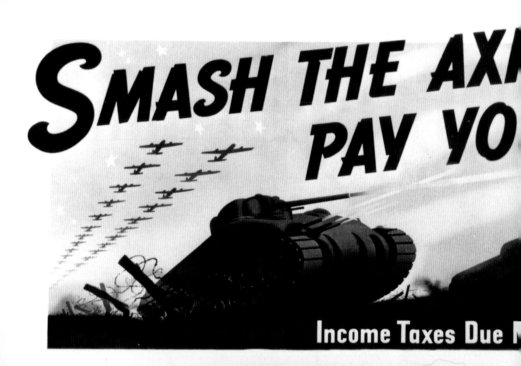

During World War II, advertisements were created to motivate U.S. citizens to pay their taxes as part of the war effort. The government required a large amount of revenue to pay for military operations abroad.

raising half of the cost of World War II via taxes fell short. Rather than 50 percent, tax revenue paid for only about 43 percent of the war cost.

TAXMEN UNDER FIRE

Roosevelt famously complained about how confusing the tax code had become, and Albert Einstein once declared that the hardest thing in the world to understand is income taxes. As people complained of the increasing complexity of taxes, Congress investigated allegations that the Bureau of Internal Revenue committed fraud, bribery, and embezzlement.

In November 1950, the California Crime Commission charged the Bureau of Internal Revenue with possible corruption. It claimed that the agency failed to prosecute tax-dodging racketeers. By 1952, after the investigative committee found evidence of major corruption, several hundred Internal Revenue employees resigned or were indicted for offenses against the tax laws.

President Harry Truman developed a sweeping reorganization of the Bureau of Internal Revenue. Rather than having top positions filled with appointees, there would now be only one in an attempt to reduce opportunities for corruption. There would be more oversight of tax employees, new procedures for handling various tax cases, and the creation on an independent Inspection Service. On July 9,

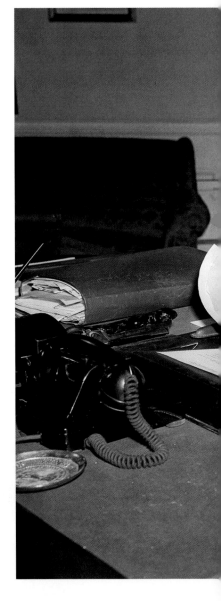

President Harry Truman and Secretary of the Treasury John W. Snyder work together to reorganize the IRS. The agency had become corrupt and untrustworthy in the 1950s.

1953, the Bureau of Internal Revenue changed its name to the Internal Revenue Service.

TAX CUTS AND POLITICS

Spending and taxation have always been linked, and many of President John F. Kennedy's economic advisers suggested spurring the economy by increasing federal spending. Instead, Kennedy elected to stimulate consumer demand by cutting taxes and putting more money back into the pockets of taxpayers. Politically, it was easier for the president to push tax cuts rather than tax increases.

Kennedy's plan included reducing the top tax rate from 91 percent to 65, and the bottom rate from 20 percent to 14. President Kennedy would not live to see his plan set into motion, so new president Lyndon B. Johnson oversaw it while slightly increasing the top rate to 70 percent.

During the 1970s, the tax-and-spend attitude of the New Deal era—with its emphasis on using tax dollars to fund social welfare programs—changed into a more conservative policy of cutting welfare programs and reducing taxes. President Richard Nixon tried to find a way to reduce the budget and cut taxes, yet continue to spend just enough to save

REAGAN SLASHES TAXES FOR THE WEALTHY

The new wave of antitax conservative Republicans led to the election of Ronald Reagan as president. In 1981, President Reagan reduced the top income tax rate from 70 to 50 percent, and the bottom rate from 14 to 11 percent. In sharp contrast with the previous era, the top rate was reduced further to 28 percent after the Tax Reform Act of 1986. Conversely, the bottom rate was raised from 11 percent back up to 14. This meant that the top income earners paid dramatically less, while the lowest earners paid significantly more under President Reagan.

the country from recession. The country began to experience high inflation—when the money supply increases along with prices, but the purchasing power of the dollar plummets. As the value of the dollar sank, cities fell into disrepair, property taxes increased in an attempt to raise funds to repair the crumbling cities, and homeowners rebelled against these higher taxes.

As the politics of taxation changed in the 1970s, the value of the dollar fell and many cities lacked money for infrastructure improvements, social programs, and public services. These tenements in the South Bronx, in New York City, reflected the harsh reality of the new economy.

The liberalism that reached new heights with President Franklin D. Roosevelt gave way to a new wave of conservatism. Various groups in the 1970s joined together to push a conservative strategy. Their main rallying points were stronger national defense, antielitism, and family values. When the IRS removed the tax-exempt status of Christian schools, conservative Christians became involved with politics for the first time and joined the conservative movement.

TAXES, SPENDING, SURPLUS, AND DEFICITS

The conservative movement's influence continued on after Reagan's presidency. It even helped limit his successor, President George H. W. Bush, to one term after he broke a campaign promise and raised the top income tax rate to 31 percent in 1990.

President Bill Clinton followed President Bush's lead
and further raised the top tax
rate to 39.6 percent in 1993.
However, he also raised the
threshold for the top tax rate
from $86,500 in income to
$250,000, or about
$400,000 today.

Conservative Republicans
feared economic apocalypse
with the tax increase, but the
opposite happened. President
Clinton reduced both spending and the deficit, while the
gross domestic product (the
monetary value of all goods
and services produced in a
country) improved. Under
eight years of President
Clinton and his fiscally conservative policy, the national
deficit was transformed into
a surplus.

President George W. Bush inherited the Clinton-era
surplus. But he saw it as a danger to the economy in
the hands of a Congress he distrusted and feared

George H. W. Bush accepted the nomination as Republican candidate for president in 1988. During his speech accepting the nomination, he made the following pledge: "Read my lips: No new taxes!" Bush was forced to break his promise and raise taxes, contributing to his failed reelection bid in 1992.

would squander it on government spending initiatives. He sought to stimulate the economy with tax cuts rather than spending. However, the surplus soon became a huge deficit when government revenue plummeted (and spending on the Iraq and Afghanistan wars soared), and the economy suffered a slump second only to the Great Depression. The so-called Great Recession that began in 2007 had been set in motion primarily by ill-advised home lending practices, dubious investment packages that bundled together risky mortgages, and the ensuing collapse of the real estate market. The decreased government spending on domestic programs, the high cost of waging two wars simultaneously, and the reduced tax revenue under President Bush helped to deepen the recession and increase its severity.

Initially, new president Barack Obama promised to end the tax cuts enacted during George W. Bush's presidency, but he extended the cuts in 2010. In 2013, the American Taxpayer Relief Act of 2012, an act that extended the tax cuts for lower-income families but ended the cuts for higher incomes, was passed.

CHAPTER SIX

TAXATION IN THE NEW MILLENNIUM

Taxation in America changed quite dramatically from the earliest days of the Sugar Act to the debates over what President Obama should do with the Bush-era tax cuts. Antitax fighters from the colonial era, such as Samuel Adams, would surely have a hard time relating to the 91 percent income tax rate set during FDR's New Deal era. But with those tax dollars, Americans have been afforded a level of comfort, convenience, health, safety, and security that would have been unimaginable to any American who ever lived in the days before the New Deal.

Taxes helped fund major public projects—such as new and improved roads, bridges, tunnels, dams, hospitals, and schools—during President Franklin D. Roosevelt's era. Today, the debate over taxpayer-funded universal health care has created more controversy. Despite the greater quality of life afforded Americans by taxpayer-funded programs and services, taxes remain a source of intense conflict and controversy.

THE DEMOCRATIC PARTY'S TAX POLICY

In 2012, the major issues in America included job creation and the sluggish economy. President Obama inherited the second largest economic crisis in American history, and much of his first term was spent addressing the prolonged and very deep recession. The Democratic Party ran on a platform that included tax cuts for middle- and lower-income earners.

Obama and his fellow Democrats highlighted the passage of the American Jobs Act, which included payroll tax relief and tax credits for businesses that hire veterans. Tax credits were also given to first-time homebuyers in order to stimulate the housing market. Democrats supported tax reform to ensure tax rates for the wealthy would remain high, while also cutting the corporate tax rate. Tax dollars would also be spent on education and easing the burden of those with student loans. The basic principle was that social welfare programs such as Social Security and Medicare would not be cut because the money to fund the programs would come from the wealthiest citizens.

President Barack Obama wanted to help unemployed Americans find work and provide tax relief to businesses with his American Jobs Act of 2011.

THE REPUBLICAN PARTY'S TAX POLICY

At this time, the Republican Party supported many of the same basic principles of cutting tax rates and simplifying the tax code that the Democratic Party did. The differences beyond these areas of agreement, however, were many.

Proposed Republican tax cuts would be flatter than those in the Democratic plan. The Republican plan was to extend the Bush tax cuts, reduce tax rates on investments for middle- and low-income taxpayers, and eliminate the estate tax. For corporations, the Republican Party wanted to improve international competitiveness by cutting corporate tax rates. They believed this would lead to greater job creation. They supported a national sales tax on the condition that it coincided with a repeal of the Sixteenth Amendment and its income tax provision, a longtime goal of American conservatives.

The Republican Party's philosophy followed Thomas Jefferson's "wise and frugal government." Similar to Nixon's and Reagan's cuts of social welfare programs, the 2012 Republican opinion viewed such programs, like Medicare, as evidence of a "big government entitlement society." The party believed taxes, like spending and regulation, should be kept to a minimum to stimulate economic growth.

OTHER POLITICAL PARTIES ON TAXES

The Tea Party is a splinter group within the Republican Party. It is a collection of different antitax groups with similar goals and no central leadership. Many politicians ran as part of the Tea Party in the 2010 races for seats in Congress and found success. However, results were less encouraging following the 2012 elections. In 2012, Tea Party–affiliated politicians called for the end of what they considered to be excessive taxation. Their belief is that taxes are a burden on the liberty guaranteed to citizens by the Constitution. The main idea is to not only slash taxes but also drastically reduce government spending.

In contrast, the Green Party platform does not call for the elimination of taxes, but rather the institution of fairer progressive taxes. The version of tax reform the Green Party argues for includes the closing of loopholes and exemptions that it believes encourages corporations and the super wealthy to avoid paying a fair and proportionate amount of taxes. Green Party members believe that exempting individuals with incomes less than $25,000—and families with incomes less than $50,000—from paying state and federal income taxes would help the economy. In effect, they argue that higher taxes among wealthy corporations and individuals and lower taxes among

The anti-tax Tea Party became a political force in 2010, when many of its candidates won congressional elections. A Tea Party rally in Chicago, Illinois, is shown here.

the working and middle classes will spur consumer spending and economic growth, while also ensuring adequate government funding of programs and services. Finally, the Green Party also supports tax changes that encourage environmentally friendly actions and impose surcharges on tobacco, alcohol, soda, and other junk food.

CHALLENGING THE AFFORDABLE CARE ACT

The government enacted the Affordable Care Act on March 23, 2010. The goal of the act was to increase the number of people with affordable access to health insurance. In 2013, the effectiveness of the act was debated as pieces of the law were slowly put into place. The money to pay for the Affordable Care Act would come from a set of new taxes and penalties on individuals, businesses, and health care providers.

The Affordable Care Act, signed into law by President Barack Obama, was designed to provide health care for all U.S. citizens. Implementation of the law did not go as smoothly as the president hoped it would, however.

The Supreme Court case *National Federation of Independent Business v. Sebelius* was a major decision regarding the Affordable Care Act. Decided by the Supreme Court on June 28, 2012, the justices ruled on two important provisions of the act. First, the act's individual mandate requires every individual to purchase a minimum level of health insurance. Second, the Medicaid expansion provision of the act requires federal funds to be given to states to pay for the health care of individuals whose income falls below a certain level.

The claim by various businesses was that requiring individuals to purchase health insurance was an unfair tax that went beyond the Constitution. Specifically, their challenge stated that the act went beyond the "necessary and proper" guidelines of the Constitution. The second part of the lawsuit said that Congress was coercing the states into adopting the Medicaid expansion under threat of withholding federal funding for the existing Medicaid.

The Court ruled that by a narrow vote of 5–4 the Affordable Care Act was not a violation of the Constitution. The individual mandate was upheld on the basis that it was not a tax but a penalty. Because it is defined as a penalty, it does not fall under the taxation rules covered by the Constitution.

The Medicaid expansion was partially upheld. The Court ruled that states may refuse the Medicaid expansion, but if they do, they will not receive the additional federal funding. The existing Medicaid funding cannot be withheld because of a state's refusal of the Affordable Care Act's Medicaid expansion.

THE IRS COURTS CONTROVERSY

In 2013, the Internal Revenue Service was accused of scrutinizing the tax-exempt applications of various groups based on their political affiliations.

Conservative groups claimed the IRS was targeting them because of their political and antitax views. Although reports showed that liberal groups received similar scrutiny, the issue was not fully resolved by year's end.

In response to the allegations, the IRS created new procedures to avoid similar situations in the future. Accountability for its actions was improved with new

In 2013, U.S. Treasury Inspector General for Tax Administration J. Russell George, former IRS Commissioner Douglas Shulman, and IRS Director of Exempt Organizations Lois Lerner testified before Congress amid allegations of misconduct.

management and a new Accountability Review Board. Improvements were made to the IRS's review process, including clearly stating the requirements for achieving tax exemption. Finally, although the investigation found no evidence of inappropriate actions, the IRS planned to undertake extra review processes and make everything transparent to the public by posting reports on the IRS.gov Web site.

FAIR TAXES

In the modern era, making sure everyone pays his or her fair share has become a big issue for taxpayers. In the New Deal era, many American corporations and individuals felt it was their duty to pay a fair share of taxes to help fund government services, projects, and programs that were of benefit to all citizens and strengthened the nation itself. Nowadays, however, tax loopholes, or special tax deals to reduce the amount of taxes one pays, are commonplace. They are especially available to and exploited by wealthy corporations and the very rich.

In 2010, the Tax Policy Center released a report that showed that many taxpayers in the top 1 percent, those with incomes greater than $350,000, paid less in federal income taxes proportionally than those in the second income quintile (those with incomes greater than $20,500). This means that the working and middle classes assume a disproportionate tax burden, while the wealthy receive a series of tax breaks and tax dodges.

Much of the political conversation and campaigns focus on "fair taxes." The marginal tax rate on the ultra-wealthy dropped from 91 percent under President Dwight D. Eisenhower in the 1950s to 36 percent in the 2000s. Warren Buffett, the third richest man in the world as of 2012, made news when he revealed that he paid 17.7 percent on his taxable income, while his secretary was taxed at 30 percent of hers.

THE FUTURE OF TAX POLICY

The modern era of America includes tax policies that were impossible to predict in the days of the Founding Fathers. One such policy debated in 2013 was the Marketplace Fairness Act. Currently, the decision in the case *National Bellas Hess v. Illinois Department of Revenue* protects retailers from a sales tax on sales made in another state. Simply put, there is no sales tax requirement for online purchases made in one state from a retailer located in another state. The Marketplace Fairness Act gives states the power to force online retailers to collect a sales tax at the time

WHAT DO TAXES PAY FOR?

Where does all the tax revenue go? Oliver Wendell Holmes Jr., a justice of the Supreme Court in the early 1900s, claimed that taxes are what we pay for civilized society. In the past, taxes were used to pay for wars and to pay off the national debt. During the New Deal era, tax money was spent on major public works projects.

The Department of the Treasury published a short report in 2009. At that time, Social Security, Medicare, and other retirement programs took the largest portion of taxes, at 34 percent. Other social programs used approximately 21 percent of the tax revenue. Twenty-two percent is given to national defense, veterans, and foreign affairs. Physical, human, and community development takes up about 15 percent, while paying off interest on the national debt uses about 5 percent. About 2 percent of taxes go to federal law enforcement and general government operation costs.

of purchase, regardless of where they are headquartered and where their customers reside.

The Internet is still relatively new technology, and only now are online taxes being introduced and challenged. The Marketplace Fairness Act was introduced in February, 2013, and it will certainly not be the last piece of legislation regarding the taxes of online sales.

As new technologies emerge, there will be tax questions regarding those as well. Different political groups will argue one way or another, and the citizens of the United States will be passionately involved in the debate. From the days of the Stamp Act to the introduction of Internet taxes, Americans have always challenged the constitutionality of taxation. Perhaps it is time to update the saying: the only guarantees in life are death, taxes, and forever unresolved debates about taxes.

GLOSSARY

amendment A formal change or addition to the U.S. Constitution.

apportion To divide and distribute among a number of people or groups.

deduction Something that can be subtracted from a total, such as income.

direct tax A tax taken directly from an individual.

dividend A share of a company's profits paid to the shareholders.

estate tax A tax on an inheritance.

excise tax An indirect tax on goods often passed on to the consumer.

gross domestic product (GDP) The total value of goods and services produced within a country's borders in a given period of time.

indirect tax A tax on goods and services.

inflation The rise in the price of goods due to an increase in the money supply over a period of time.

sectionalism Restricting one's interest to one's particular region or group.

tariff A tax on imports or exports.

taxation A charge a citizen pays to help fund government operations, services, programs, and projects.

tax credit An amount subtracted from how much a person owes in taxes.

taxpayer A person who must pay a tax.

wage The amount of money a person is paid in exchange for work.

FOR MORE INFORMATION

Canada Revenue Agency (CRA)
555 MacKenzie Avenue, 7th floor
Ottawa, ON K1A 0L5
Canada
(800) 267-6999
Web site: http://www.cra-arc.gc.ca
This national tax organization administers tax laws for
   Canada and most of its provinces and territories.

Canadian Tax Foundation (CTF)
595 Bay Street, Suite 1200
Toronto, ON M5G 2N5
Canada
(416) 599-0CTF (0283)
Web site: http://www.ctf.ca
This is a nonprofit organization that provides infor-
   mation and education on tax issues.

Free File Alliance
7137 Main Street, Suite B
Clifton, VA 20124
Web site: http://freefile.irs.gov
The Free File Alliance is a nonprofit coalition of tax
   software companies that has partnered with the
   IRS to help Americans prepare and e-file their fed-
   eral tax returns for free.

Internal Revenue Service (IRS)
Metro Plex 1
8401 Corporate Drive, Suite 300
Landover, MD 20785
(800) 829-1040
Web site: http://www.irs.gov
The IRS is the U.S. government agency responsible for
tax collection and tax law enforcement.

Tax Analysts
400 South Maple Avenue, Suite 400
Falls Church, VA 22046
(800) 955-2444
Web site: http://www.taxanalysts.com
This is a nonprofit organization that provides tax
analysis and news. Included on its Web site is the
Tax History Museum and Tax History Project.

Treasury Inspector General for Tax Administration
1401 H Street NW, Suite 469
Washington, DC 20005
(202) 622-1090
Web site: http://www.treasury.gov
Established under the IRS Restructuring and Reform
Act of 1998, the Treasury Inspector provides inde-
pendent oversight of IRS activities.

U.S. Department of the Treasury
1500 Pennsylvania Avenue NW
Washington, DC 20220
(202) 622-2000
Web site: http://www.treasury.gov
The U.S. Department of the Treasury is a governmental agency with the role of promoting economic security, financial prosperity, and job creation in the United States.

WEB SITES

Due to the changing nature of Internet links, Rosen Publishing has developed an online list of Web sites related to the subject of this book. This site is updated regularly. Please use this link to access the list:

http://www.rosenlinks.com/UUSC/Tax

FOR FURTHER READING

Acton, Johnny, and David Goldblatt. *Eyewitness Economy*. New York, NY: DK, 2010.

Baten, Linda. *Taxes, Taxes, Taxes*. West Vancouver, BC, Canada: Scripts for Schools, 2012.

Bolden, Tonya. *Alphabet Soup: New Deal America, 1932–1939*. New York, NY: Alfred A. Knopf, 2010.

Clifford , Tim. *Our Economy in Action*. Vero Beach, FL: Rourke Publishing, 2009.

De Capua, Sarah. *Paying Taxes*. Danbury, CT: Children's Press, 2013.

Engdahl, Sylvia. *Welfare*. Detroit, MI: Gale Cengage Learning, 2011.

Fradin, Dennis B. *The Stamp Act of 1765*. New York, NY: Marshall Cavendish Benchmark, 2010.

Freedman, Russell, and Peter Malone. *The Boston Tea Party*. New York, NY: Holiday House, 2012.

Gondosch, Linda. *How Did Tea and Taxes Spark a Revolution? and Other Questions About the Boston Tea Party*. Minneapolis, MN: Lerner Publications, 2011.

Judson, Karen. *The Constitution of the United States*. Berkeley Heights, NJ: Enslow, 2013.

La Bella, Laura. *How Taxation Works*. New York, NY: Rosen Publishing, 2011.

Magoon, Kekla. *The Welfare Debate*. Edina, MN: ABDO, 2009.

Nichols, Clive. *Taxes and Government Spending*. New York, NY: Rosen Publishing, 2011.

Orr, Tamra. *A Kid's Guide to the Economy*. Hockessin, DE: Mitchell Lane Publishers, 2010.

Piper, Mike. *Taxes Made Simple: Income Taxes Explained in 100 Pages or Less*. St. Louis, MO: Simple Subjects, 2009.

Young, Mitchell. *Social Security*. Detroit, MI: Greenhaven Press, 2010.

BIBLIOGRAPHY

Adams, C. *Those Dirty Rotten Taxes: The Tax Revolts That Built America*. New York, NY: Free Press, 1998.

Bank, S. A. *Anglo-American Corporate Taxation: Tracing the Common Roots of Divergent Approaches*. New York, NY: Cambridge University Press, 2011.

Bartlett, B. R. *The Benefit and the Burden: Tax Reform—Why We Need It and What It Will Take*. New York, NY: Simon & Schuster, 2012.

Brookhiser, R. *James Madison*. New York, NY: Basic Books, 2011.

Democrats.org. "2012 Democratic National Platform: Moving America Forward." Retrieved September 2013 (http://www.democrats.org/ democratic-national-platform).

Freehling, W. W. *Prelude to Civil War: The Nullification Controversy in South Carolina, 1816–1836*. New York, NY: Oxford University Press, 1992.

GOP.com. "2012 Republican Platform." Retrieved September 2013 (http://www.gop.com/wp-content/ uploads/2012/08/2012GOPPlatform.pdf).

GP.org. "The Green Party of the United States." Retrieved September 2013 (http://www.gp.org/ committees/platform/2012).

Hall, K. L. *The Oxford Guide to United States Supreme Court Decisions*. New York, NY: Oxford University Press, 1999.

Internal Revenue Service. "Affordable Care Act Tax Provisions." Retrieved September 2013 (http://www.irs.gov/uac/Affordable-Care-Act-Tax-Provisions).

Internal Revenue Service. *IRS Historical Fact Book: A Chronology, 1646–1992*. Washington, DC: Dept. of the Treasury, 1993.

Internal Revenue Service. "Report Outlines Changes for IRS to Ensure Accountability, Chart a Path Forward; Immediate Actions, Next Steps Outlined." June 24, 2013. Retrieved September 2013 (http://www.irs.gov/uac/Newsroom/Report-Outlines-Changes-for-IRS-To-Ensure-Accountability,-Chart-a-Path-Forward;-Immediate-Actions,-Next-Steps-Outlined).

Internal Revenue Service. "Why Do I Have to Pay Taxes?" Retrieved September 2013 (http://www.irs.gov/pub/irs-pdf/p2105.pdf).

MarketplaceFairness.org. "What Is the Marketplace Fairness Act of 2013?" Retrieved September 2013 (http://www.marketplacefairness.org/what-is-the-marketplace-fairness-act).

Marshall, J., and J. P. Cotton. *The Constitutional Decisions of John Marshall*. New York, NY: G. P. Putnam's Sons, 1905.

Mckenna, M. C. *Franklin Roosevelt and the Great Constitutional War: The Court-Packing Crisis of 1937.* New York, NY: Fordham University Press, 2002.

Morgan, E. S. *The Birth of the Republic, 1763–89.* Chicago, IL: University of Chicago Press, 1992.

Popkin, W. D. *Introduction to Taxation.* Newark, NJ: LexisNexis, 2008.

Powell, T. R. *Vagaries and Varieties in Constitutional Interpretation.* Union, NJ: Lawbook Exchange, 2002.

Reich, J. R. *Colonial America.* Englewood Cliffs, NJ: Prentice Hall, 1994.

Richards, L. L. *Shays's Rebellion: The American Revolution's Final Battle.* Philadelphia, PA: University of Pennsylvania Press, 2002.

Rodgers, P. *United States Constitutional Law: An Introduction.* Jefferson, NC: McFarland, 2011.

Schulman, B. J. *The Seventies: The Great Shift in American Culture, Society, and Politics.* New York, NY: Free Press, 2001.

Stone, O., and P. J. Kuznick. *The Untold History of the United States.* New York, NY: Gallery Books, 2011.

TeaParty-Platform.com. "Tea Party Movement Platform." Retrieved September 2013 (http://www.teaparty-platform.com).

Thorndike, Joseph J. "An Army of Officials: The Civil War Bureau of Internal Revenue." Social Science Research Network, December 24, 2001. Retrieved September 2013 (http://papers.ssrn.com/sol3/papers.cfm?abstract_id=294824).

Wills, G. *A Necessary Evil: A History of American Distrust of Government.* New York, NY: Simon & Schuster, 1999.

INDEX

ABOUT THE AUTHOR

Jeff Mapua is a writer living in Texas who has written on other subjects relating to politics, government, finance, and society, including books on Bill and Hillary Clinton and crowdfunding.

PHOTO CREDITS